# Folk Wisdom From Hawai'i

# Folk Wisdom From Hawai'i

## *or Don't Take Bananas*

## *On a Boat*

By Ann Kondo Corum

THE BESS PRESS
P.O. BOX 22388
HONOLULU, HAWAII 96822

*To Eric Schiff . . .*
*Thank You for the Inspiration*

**Library of Congress Cataloging in Publication Data**
CATALOG CARD NO.: 84-73554
Corum, Ann Kondo
  Folk Wisdom from Hawai'i or Don't Take Bananas on a Boat
Honolulu, Hawaii: Bess Press, Inc.
120 pages

ISBN: 0-935848-32-0
Copyright ©1985 by Ann Kondo Corum

Cover: Ann Kondo Corum
Design: Roger Eggers
Typesetting: Stats 'n Graphics
Cover Photo by B. Yonamine

# CONTENTS

# Preface

The spark for this book came from a simple statement made by a Mainland haole who was curious about some of Hawai'i's local customs and beliefs. Thinking back, I began to remember various superstitions, customs, and bits of folk wisdom from my childhood, the sometimes unexplained truisms that we in Hawai'i hold sacred. Everyone has notions (and sometimes nonsense) he believes in. Talking to family, friends, and even complete strangers, I have collected bits of "tribal truths" from people of different ethnic groups who delved into the recesses of their various backgrounds.

Basically, this book contains three types of "wisdom." The first category includes local customs – practices common to this particular locale. These are things that we do and accept without explanation.

The second category of "wisdom" is that of superstition. Superstitions have been with man since earliest times. Generally, they imply a belief in, fear of, or reverence of the unknown or the mysterious. That is to say fear often dictates an action. Whether we realize it or not, almost everybody, even the most educated person, has been at one time or other fascinated by superstitions.

The last category of "wisdom" is that of local beliefs or credoes. The word "credo" orginally stems from the Latin for "I believe." However, over the years, credo has come to mean any widely held piece of wisdom or advice which may be partially true, predominantly wrong, or even totally wrong.

Credoes are present in every culture, and the ethnically mixed society of Hawai'i offers a wealth of miscellaneous advice and beliefs.

The origin of the "wisdom" in this book is generally not known, although some bits of advice are commonly attributed to a certain ethnic group. Many overlap, with small variations, into other ethnic groups. No attempt has been made to explain the source or origin of the customs, superstitions, and credoes within the book. Whether or not they are true is irrelevant. In this collection I have merely attempted to record some local beliefs and perceptions and to convey to the reader some light-hearted whimsy and silliness.

I would like to thank all the people who contributed their bits of "wisdom" to this book. I hope the book makes you smile!

*Ann Kondo Corum*

# Practical Advice

*Always remove your shoes before entering a local house.*

*Put jars filled with water on your lawn to keep dogs off the grass.*

*If an unmarried woman steps over a broom lying on the floor she is doomed to be an old maid.*

*When you want unwanted guests to go home stand a broom on its handle.*

*If you sweep after dark you will sweep out good fortune.*

*Do not clean house on New Year's Day . . . you will sweep out good luck for the year.*

*The first thing you say on New Year's Day will come to you throughout the year.*

*If a friend gives you a gift of food in a plate, bowl, or tray you should return the container with something in it . . . never empty.*

*It is bad luck to pass food from chopstick to chopstick.*

*It is bad luck to pour tea backhanded out of the teapot.*

*A child who dreams of falling a long way has grown during the night.*

*If you dream about losing your tooth, take a tooth of a comb and flush it down the toilet to prevent bad luck.*

*Don't sit in a seat that somebody has warmed because you will end up fighting with that person.*

14

*The front door and back door of your house should not be aligned with each other because luck will walk in one door and out the other.*

*Wearing jade jewelry will keep you healthy and bring you good luck.*

*Do not take anything from a heiau (ancient Hawaiian place of worship). It will only bring you bad luck.*

*Do not take lava rock away from Hawai'i. It will bring you bad luck.*

*Madame Pele sometimes tries to hitch a ride near the volcanoes. If you see a beautiful girl or an old woman with hair the color of ashes, be sure to give her a ride to avoid bad luck.*

*Don't take pork over the Pali at night; you will have car trouble or bad luck.*

*Hilo version: Don't take pork on the Saddle Road at night. You will have bad luck.*

*Maui version: Don't take pork home with you after midnight . . . if you do, your car will stall.*

*When you think it is going to rain (and don't want it to rain), spit on a rock.*

*Rain and sun at the same time is known as "obake rain" (ghost rain).*

*Any celebration accompanied by a little rain is blessed.*

"Yakudoshi" is considered a bad luck year by Japanese. For women it is 33 (32 in American years); for men it is 41 (40 in American years). (Japanese are considered one year old at birth.) Some people have a special party to chase away bad luck. Although "Yakudoshi" is Japanese in origin, many orientals celebrate this birthday.

BANZAI!

*Many Orientals celebrate the 61st birthday (60th in American years) because they enter on a new lease on life . . . a second childhood. Red is worn by the birthday person.*

25

At Filipino weddings guests place rolled up money in the bride's lips while she dances with the groom. She then passes the money to the groom's lips.

# The Plant Kingdom

*Plant ti leaves around your house to keep the evil spirits away.*

*To rid your house of evil spirits, call a priest to bless it with holy water and ti leaves.*

*A gift wrapped in ti leaves is given in good faith. Ti leaves keep evil thoughts and spirits away.*

*If a money tree (dracaena) grows taller than the roof of your house you will never have to worry about money.*

*Don't pick flowers after dark because they are asleep.*

32

*A woman wearing a flower behind her right ear indicates she is looking for a man. A woman wearing a flower over her left ear indicates she is taken.*

Do not pick lehua blossoms or wear a lehua lei when going to Kilauea, because it will surely rain.

*Give a hala lei to wipe away misfortune.*

*Do not give a hala lei to a person campaigning for public office because it will bring on his defeat.*

*Give a hala lei to mark the completion of a venture and a beginning of a new one.*

*The maile lei is associated with courtship and love.*

*White carnation leis are usually given to women; red carnation leis to men. White represents femininity and red represents boldness, strength, and power.*

*Avoid giving a lei with the ends tied together to a pregnant woman. The circle formed may strangle the unborn child.*

*If a lei cast overboard by a visitor leaving on a ship is carried to shore by the current, he will return to Hawai'i someday.*

*Give a lei to mark memorable moments of life . . . it says hello, goodbye, thank you, congratulations, I love you . . . it says aloha.*

# Creatures In Your Life

*It is bad luck to kill a seagull.*

*When seagulls fly inland it is a sign of rain.*

*If you step on a spider it will rain tomorrow.*

*A spider appearing in the evening is a bad sign, but a spider appearing in the morning is a good sign.*

*A cricket in the house brings good luck.*

*If a big black moth comes to your house do not kill it. It is the soul of a deceased dear one coming back to visit.*

After cleaning your ears be sure creatures such as insects, mice, lizards, etc., don't eat your ear wax . . . that will make you deaf.

*If you get a bee sting make a cross in the dirt with your finger, take a pinch of dirt from the center of the cross and put it on the sting. This will prevent swelling.*

51

*Eating ants will make you strong.*

*Eating ants off the sidewalk will improve your eyesight.*

*Killing a ladybug will bring bad luck.*

*If you kill a praying mantis it will come back in the night, snatch the hair off your head and make you "bolo-head" (bald).*

*If you break off a lizard's tail, cover your ears because the
tail will jump into your ears.*

# Fishy Stuff

*Offer a lei of limu kala (common yellow-brown seaweed) to the altar of the fish god if you want good fishing or to be favored by the sea.*

*For good luck in fishing spit on your lure.*

*Don't take bananas on a boat . . . you won't catch any fish.*

*When you go fishing throw back the first fish you catch,*
*then you will have good luck catching fish that day.*

*If you get a fish bone stuck in your throat, put a fish bone on your head and swallow a lump of rice. The fish bone in your throat will dissolve.*

*Eating fish heads or fish eyeballs will increase your brain power.*

*If you eat weke (goatfish) heads you will have awful nightmares.*

# Bodily Advice

*If you steal money a rash will appear on your hands.*

To remove a wart, rub a cut nasubi* (Japanese eggplant) on it. Bury the nasubi in the ground and the wart will go away.

Hilo version: After rubbing the nasubi on the wart, throw it into the street. The first person to walk past it will catch the wart.

*Haoles use potato.

*Specks on your fingernails mean you will be getting a present soon.*

*Rubbing your fingernails together will make hair grow on your head.*

*Don't clip your fingernails or toenails at night. If you do, you won't be present when your parents die.*

*A person who peeps will get a mebo (sty) on his eye.*

*People with fat or thick earlobes will be wealthy.*

*Small ears indicate a stingy person.*

*Pigeon-toed people are stingy.*

*Baldness is a sign of prosperity.*

*If your second toe is longer than your big toe, you will be successful in life.*

*If your second toe is longer than your big toe you will*
*wear the pants in the family.*

*Itchy ears mean somebody is talking stink (saying bad things) about you.*

*An itchy right ear means good news will come; an itchy left ear means bad luck will follow.*

*People who have a beauty spot under their lower eyelid will have much sorrow in life.*

*Men whose eyebrows meet are fortunate and trouble will never come near them.*

A child with more than one giri-giri (cowlick) is a naughty child.

*Teeth wide apart mean you will be lucky, wealthy, and travel far.*

*Don't expose your belly button when it thunders because the thunder god will take it away.*

*To prevent seasickness tape an ume (Japanese pickled plum) in your belly button.*

*If you pick your belly button, you will get a belly ache.*

# New Life
# And Death

An unborn child that is "carried high" is a girl; one that is "carried low" is a boy.

*A person who keeps a toilet clean will have beautiful children.*

*A child born at the time of a full moon will always be strong.*

*If a child looks between his legs, he will soon have a brother or sister.*

*Do not walk over a child who is lying down. If you do, he will be short. To break the spell, cross over again.*

*If your baby cries at night he or she might be getting day and night mixed up. Take a picture of a rooster and pin it upside down over the baby's bed.*

*A pregnant woman whose nose becomes flat and broad will have a boy.*

*If a person's picture falls he will die soon.*

*Do not sleep with your head toward the north because you may die while asleep.*

*Do not sleep with your feet pointed toward the door because traditionally the dead are laid with their feet toward the door to help the soul depart.*

*Don't attend a funeral when pregnant . . . your baby might die.*

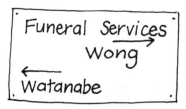

*Traditionally, the immediate family of deceased Japanese wears black clothing to the funeral while the immediate family of deceased Chinese and Koreans wears white.*

During a funeral all the windows and doors of the dead person's house must be open so that the spirit of the dead will pass through and depart.

*Leave a light burning in a deceased person's house until he is buried. The light from his house will lead him to heaven.*

*To help the spirit of the deceased depart for heaven, roll a watermelon out of the front door of his house.*

*After a person dies his personal clothing (socks, pajamas, underwear) are burned . . . never given away (Chinese).*

*After a person dies, taking his old clothes will bring you good luck (Japanese).*

*After returning from a funeral, the family of the deceased wash their feet with water boiled with leaves of guava or pomelo to purify themselves (Filipino).*

*Wash your eyes with water and pomelo leaves after returning from a funeral to wash sadness away (Chinese).*

*When you come home from a funeral sprinkle salt on yourself before entering the house to purify yourself.*

*Jump over a fire when you come home from a funeral to keep the dead from following (Chinese).*

**108**

When you make musubi (rice balls) make them triangular shaped, not round. Round musubi are made for funerals only.

*When you leave a cemetery don't look back.*

*Don't point in a cemetery. If you do, bite your finger.*

*Don't whistle at night . . . it attracts ghosts.*

*Ghosts that float can harm you, but those that walk are harmless.*

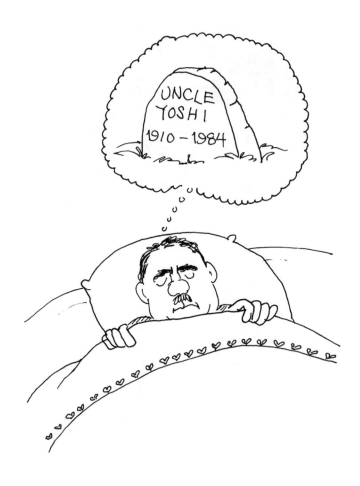

*If you dream that a person died, he will have a long life.*